Nigel

story by
Debra K. Duel

illustrated by
Lori Kiplinger Pandy

Nigel

By

Debbie Duel
Illustrated by Lori Kiplinger Pandy

Published by
Operation Outreach-USA Press
Holliston, Massachusetts

ISBN 978-0-9792144-4-8
ISBN 0-9792144-4-0

Printed in the United States of America

For Max and Natalie, the children who love Nigel the most,
and Nigel, the most wonderful dog,
who loves everyone unconditionally.

This is Nigel.

And this is Nigel's Story

Nigel lives with his family....
a mom, a dad, a teenage girl,
and a boy named Max.

Max loves Nigel more than he loves baseball, soccer or bike riding.

Nigel also lives with four cats....
Gladys, an old-lady cat.

Micky Dean, a plump,
round orange tabby.

Merl, a playful brown tabby, who loves Nigel more than he loves catnip, crunchy treats or pouncing on Micky Dean.

And, Big Bruce, an enormous gray and white cat who does not love Nigel at all.

Nigel loves everyone, even Big Bruce.
He loves his family. He loves the children at Max's bus stop.

He loves the children at Max's baseball and soccer games.
And, he loves every person and dog he meets on the street.

Nigel likes to meet his friends in the park. The people stand around and talk while the dogs play. Nigel loves playing with his friends, even the ones who play very, very rough.

Nigel plays with Gus, Ozzie, Louie, Clyde, Abby and any other dog who shows up. The dogs play, run and chase.

After awhile Nigel plunks down in a mud puddle and watches his friends run and chase.

Nigel is a young dog, but he gets tired and likes to rest -- particularly in the mud. "He doesn't have a care in the world," someone says.

"Nigel, the King of the park," another person chuckles. "What a good life. Play hard and lie in the mud!"

BUT NIGEL'S LIFE WAS NOT ALWAYS GOOD.

A long time ago, Nigel was treated very badly.
A woman kept him, but she did not take care of him.
She didn't give Nigel lots of love and attention.
She didn't provide him with lots of good, healthy food to eat. She didn't give him plenty of fresh, clean water to drink.

Instead, she tied him up to a porch railing.

The woman left him there in the cold....

all alone, with nothing to eat,

nothing to drink,

and no one

to play

with.

One day someone drove by and saw Nigel.

He stopped his car and
called the animal shelter.

"It's an emergency,
come quick!" he said.

An Officer arrived in no time. She untied a very thin, but happy dog.

Nigel wagged his tail and shook his skinny body from side to side.

His bony tail slapped the Officer's leg.

He quickly gobbled up the food the Officer gave him.

His tail wagged harder.

The Officer drove straight to the animal hospital.

Nigel is a Labrador retriever. He should weigh 75 pounds – at least.

The scale stopped at just 48!

The veterinarian told the Officer to feed Nigel five small meals a day for several weeks.

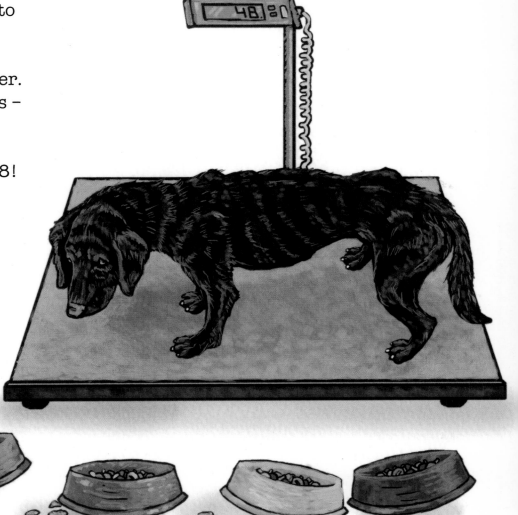

When Nigel was released from the hospital, the Officer took him to the animal shelter.

And, that's where Nigel's family saw him and fell in love.

The family adopted Nigel and took him home.

He had a bed in Max's room and a bed in the parents' room.

There were lots of toys to squeak and tear apart.

He had delicious treats and lots and lots of yummy food to eat and plenty of clean water to drink.

Life was perfect.
Well almost......

Five days a week,
Nigel walked to the
bus stop and watched Max leave.

The children at the bus stop loved Nigel.

And he loved them.

He missed them terribly when they left for school.

When the bus driver pulled away from the curb, Nigel would lie down on the concrete and refuse to move.

He wanted the children to come back.

He wanted them to give him lots of pats and belly rubs.

When Nigel finally agreed to go home, he would plop down on his bed in Max's room.
He looked so sad.
Nigel was **bored.**

The mom took him outside and tossed the ball.

She begged Nigel to fetch the ball, but Nigel didn't move.

The mom sighed. She picked up the ball and took Nigel inside.

Nigel went back to bed.

Later, the mom tried to take Nigel for a walk.
Nigel refused to leave the porch.

No way.

He would not walk around the neighborhood
during school hours.

The mom gave up. She let Nigel in the house.
He went back to bed and the mom took a walk
by herself.

But later in the afternoon, Nigel DID want to go
for a walk. He knew just when the school bus
would be returning.

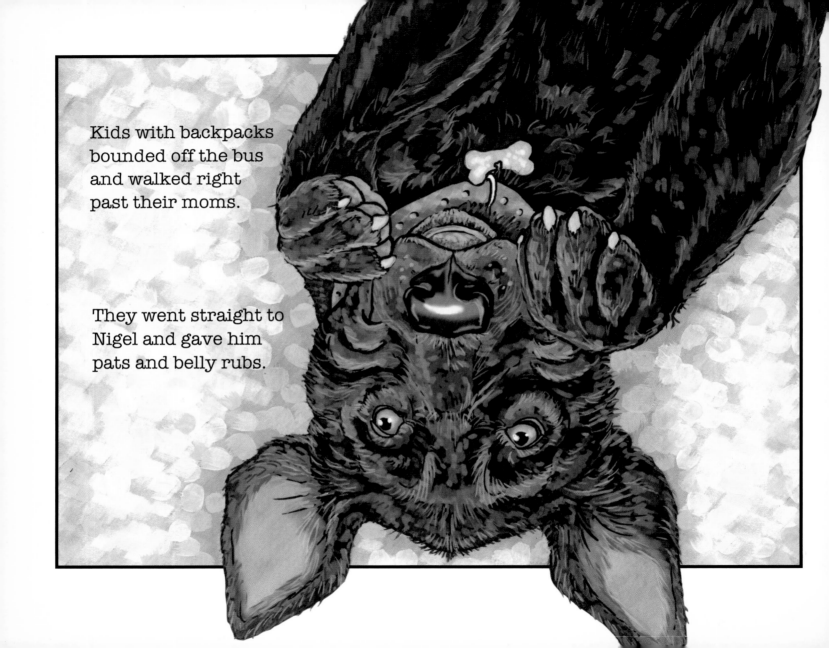

Kids with backpacks
bounded off the bus
and walked right
past their moms.

They went straight to
Nigel and gave him
pats and belly rubs.

He wagged his tail very fast
hitting every one of the
children as if he were saying,

"WELCOME HOME."

Nigel really missed the kids when they were gone, and kids are gone a lot.

They go to school, to friends' houses, to dance classes and soccer games.

Nigel loved the children in his home, and all other children, too.

He wanted to hang around kids all the time, any kids would do.

The mom knew this and started
thinking of ways to help Nigel.

She thought long and hard and then
came up with a great idea.

Nigel could work at the library.

THE LIBRARY?!

What could a dog do in a library?

Something very special.

Nigel became a Reading Buddy.

He listens while children read to him. The reader and Nigel sit in a cozy spot. Nigel likes looking at the pictures.

He's a very good listener.

Nigel makes the children smile, even when they stumble over the words.

When they have trouble, Nigel wags his tail and pokes the child with his nose. It's like he's saying, "Come on, you can do it."

Nigel likes all of the books, particularly the ones about dogs. And, the readers give lots of pats and belly rubs.

This makes Nigel VERY happy!

Maybe one day someone will write a
book about Nigel and read it to all of
the children who love dogs.

And, maybe a dog just like Nigel will
listen to the story and enjoy a
belly rub, a pat and a hug.

Photo by Ed Bernstein

The End

In 2004, the Washington Humane Society responded to 1,752 reports of animal cruelty. Nigel's rescue is a result of one of those calls. Today, he is in a permanent, loving home. Nigel likes sharing his story with children because it teaches them that every one of us can help animals. As a "reading buddy" for the Washington Animal Rescue League, Nigel now helps children become better readers.

About Operation Outreach–USA

Operation Outreach–USA (OO-USA) provides free literacy and character education programs to elementary and middle schools across the country.

Because reading is the gateway to success, leveling the learning field for at-risk children is critical. By giving books to students to own, confidence is built and motivated readers are created. OO-USA selects books with messages that teach compassion, respect and determination. OO-USA involves the school and the home with tools for teachers and parents to nurture and guide children as they learn and grow.

More than one million children in schools in all fifty states have participated in the program thanks to the support of a broad alliance of corporate, foundation and individual sponsors.

To learn more about Operation Outreach–USA and how to help, visit www.oousa.org, call 1-800-243-7929, or email info@oousa.org.

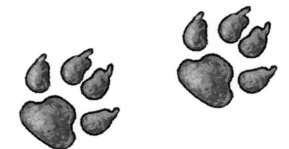